"Its time has come! Fr. John Forliti's book responds creatively to the hopes and fears, questions and concerns of contemporary young adults. His insights, observations, and suggestions speak directly and pertinently to the reader. The vision, values, and virtues he shares will contribute significantly to the growth of the young men and women who are searching for meaning and relevance in a truly complex and challenging age."

Rev. James F. Hawker
Vicar for Education
Diocese of Charlotte, NC

"*Straight Talk for Young Adults: About Faith and Values* is exactly that—a slim, succinct volume that today's young adults can wrap their thoughts around. No punches pulled, Fr. Forliti, using his many years of university student services work, consistently goes directly to the point. Especially attractive is the book's format, using classic Catholic categories like commandments and sacraments, giving them a fresh insight."

Rev. Geo. M. Schroeder
Veteran Campus Minister

"This book makes a significant contribution to the goal of guiding young adults toward Catholic faith and values. Father Forliti draws on contemporary examples and personal experiences and molds these into a readable, well constructed book that will hold young readers' attention. This is a highly pertinent and useful book that fulfills its title's promise."

Bruce F. Vento
Member of Congress

"*Straight Talk for Young Adults* takes a unique approach to dealing with five important topics, presenting succinct distillations of insights on values, God's law, faith, love and sexuality, and virtues. The author's personal reflections in this book encourage his readers 'to go deeper rather than wider' in their search for meaning—a search which may well lead, he suggests, to the discovery 'of the heart of God.'

"True to his promise of 'straight talk,' Forliti tackles several themes that are not popular in our culture and demonstrates well that 'deep in the heart of the Christian message is the belief that we are expected to take responsibility for our lives and our actions' and challenges young adults to 'listen to the God within.'"

Catherine McNamee, CSJ
Institute for Social Thought and Management
University of St. Thomas

"*Straight Talk for Young Adults: About Faith and Values* presents a valuable and moving guide to the human and spiritual issues confronting young adults from all faith traditions. Weaving together story, parable, wisdom, and advice, this special work touches the heart and sparks the kind of self-examination necessary for finding one's way in the world.

"Fr. John Forliti writes with passion. As teacher, priest, scholar, administrator, and friend, his ministry has focused on the adolescent and young adult journey. No one knows this audience better. *Straight Talk for Young Adults: About Faith and Values* is ideal for individual reflection or small group discussion. I hope it finds its way into the lives of all young adults and those who connect with them."

Peter L. Benson, Ph.D.
President, Search Institute

Straight Talk
for
Young Adults

About Faith
& Values

REV. JOHN FORLITI

TWENTY-THIRD PUBLICATIONS
Mystic, CT 06355

Twenty-Third Publications
185 Willow Street
P.O. Box 180
Mystic, CT 06355
(860) 536-2611
800-321-0411

ISBN 0-89622-735-9
Library of Congress Catalog Card Number 97-60727
Printed in the U.S.A.

Acknowledgments

Thanks to those who served as readers. Their comments and critiques were invaluable: Jeri Rockett, Alan Sickbert, Sr. Sharon Howell, Elaine Foell, Mike Lentz, Glen Meyer, Jerome Gerber, Paul Timmins, Mark Quayle, Mike Roach, Dan Cavanaugh, Kim Hastings, Jared Morris, Beth DeZiel, Kristin Tupa, and Jared Opatz.

Contents

Introduction   1

STRAIGHT TALK ABOUT
Values

1   Up Front   5
2   Warren   7
3   Where Did You End Up?   9
4   Self-Esteem   11
5   Unexpected Love   13
6   Making A Difference   15
7   Be A Friend   17
8   Giving Our Word   19

STRAIGHT TALK ABOUT
God's Law

9   False Gods   23
10   First Things First   25
11   Sunday Priorities   27
12   What Is Honor?   29
13   God Is Love   31
14   Nothing Hurts as Much   33
15   Give It Back   35
16   Tell the Truth   37
17   Wrong Desires   39
18   Greedy Hearts   41

STRAIGHT TALK ABOUT
Faith

19	Close the Gap	45
20	Times Have Changed	47
21	God Deserves the Best!	49
22	Christ and Christmas	51
23	Plans for Lent	53
24	About Marriage	55
25	The Call to Priesthood	57
26	What about Sin?	59

STRAIGHT TALK ABOUT
Love and Sexuality

27	Intimacy	63
28	Adolescent Sex	65
29	Living Together	67
30	Peer Pressure	69
31	Men Who Rape	71
32	Acquaintance Rape	73

STRAIGHT TALK ABOUT
Virtues

33	Let Goodness Guide You	77
34	Be Courageous	79
35	Practice Tolerance	80
36	Show Integrity	81
37	Keep Commitments	82
38	Be Good Stewards	83
39	Show Reverence	84
40	Respect Yourself	85

Straight
Talk
for
Young
Adults

Introduction

Dear Young Adult,

As you move into your next phase of life, you will probably treasure more than ever whatever insights you can gain about the meaning of life. Childhood has its special tasks, so does adolescence, but these earliest stages of human development are filled with introductions and discoveries, somewhat like the butterfly leaving its cocoon and circling around to taste the flavors in the open spaces. Toward the end of the teen years, many young people develop a keener desire for meaning.

The reflections in this book are offered as a help in your search for the meaning of life. They arise out of our shared Catholic heritage and reflect the bumps along the way that at least this one Christian traveler has experienced. We need not travel life's journey alone, nor walk its pathways as though no one has gone before us. We can benefit from the wisdom of the ages and the insights of the sages. What I have attempted to bring together in these reflections are distillations of insights given to me. I have come to believe that very often in life insights are the most valuable treasures we can receive.

As you ponder these pages, strive to go deeper rather than wider. Take your time, let silence be your companion, listen to the voice of God within. You are the artwork of the creator of the world. Reverence your soul and your body—you are made in the image of God and your value is beyond measure. Value is meaning. As you discover the true meaning of life, you will discover the heart of God.

STRAIGHT TALK ABOUT
Values

1

Up Front

I still chuckle whenever I think about it. My grandnephew, Mario, aged 5, had taken scissors to his hair and lopped off a lock right up front! "What did you do?" his devastated mother asked. Thinking for a long moment over the nature of his act, the little guy grew an innocent smile on his face and replied, "I must have lost my mind for a minute!"

Adam blamed Eve. Eve blamed the serpent. The serpent couldn't defend himself, took the rap, and has had a bad name ever since. Adam and Eve exhibited a behavior all too familiar and common with us humans; they would not accept responsibility for their deeds. They tried to pass on the blame. We see it all the time, in ourselves, in public figures, in students of all ages and sizes, at work, at home, at church, at school.

Deep in the heart of the Christian message is the belief that we are expected to take responsibility for our lives and our actions. Thanks to parents who believe this and to teachers who care enough to teach it and to preachers who preach it, most of us grow up and out of that "blame others" mentality. Eventually we realize that honesty is the best policy. Gradually we learn that only those sins can be forgiven which are truly admitted and accurately assigned.

It makes for a better world when people take responsibility for their lives. For example, nothing delights a teacher's heart more than students who 'fess up to their misguided behaviors and face the music. Did you do it or didn't you? Yes or No. Cut the dancing around, take responsibility for your choices and behaviors, take the consequences you deserve, and let's all move on! Save the game-playing for the athletic field. Sooner or later, we learn that passing the buck is an exercise in futility. Eventually, we have to face the music. Why not right up front?

Warren

Warren was a likable kid, full of fun and vitality. He was 18 when he died, a freshman in college, at the beginning of Thanksgiving break. It had been a bad year for colleges in Minnesota. Two intoxicated students from a university fell asleep on railroad tracks and were run over. Another student from another college died from alcohol poisoning. He consumed 18 straight shots of whiskey, passed out in the bar, and was brought back to the dorm and put to bed by his friends. Within a half hour he was dead.

All four deaths were related to alcohol. Warren reportedly had been drinking in several spots that fateful Wednesday night, including at a local bar (since closed) and with older collegians. Alone in his car, with a blood alcohol level of .2, he careened down a quiet neighborhood street, flew over the embankment, and sank in the river. Thanksgiving Day he failed to show up for dinner with his family. It was Saturday before the police put bits of evidence together and found his body.

Some of his classmates decided to rent a bus and go to his funeral. As they were preparing for the trip, several of the guys decided to purchase a keg of beer for consumption on the road! Not surprisingly, when college staff heard this they intervened. There would be no alcohol on that bus! The irony of this was incredible.

I promised to keep Warren's memory alive in the hope that a similar tragedy might never happen again. Alcohol is a drug that kills thousands of young people every year. Sadly, it's too commonplace, too normal a part of our lives. Why do intelligent, bright, wonderful kids refuse to acknowledge its death-dealing potential?

Where Did You End Up?

It happened at a homecoming game. Our college was pitted against our number one rival. I overheard a conversation between two female students sitting in the row behind me.

One asked the other, "Where did you end up last night?" "I don't know!" came the reply. As they talked, it became clear that both had gotten "hammered" as part of the homecoming celebration. "I was going to stop at one drink," the first student said.

My heart turned sad. Racing through my mind were the ugly possibilities. Blacked out, how could they have protected themselves from being exploited, raped, or violated? Would they ever know how close they might have come to causing more carnage on the highways, by driving "under the influence"?

Young adults, taking risks that might easily ruin their lives, are toying with fire that can and does destroy their innocence, not to mention their futures. What's wrong with their consciences that they take the gift of life so lightly? Why do they behave as though life were not a gift and a responsibility?

Nobody enjoys the company of a drunk! Even the nicest people can do the grossest things when "drinking." Public urination, foul language, vandalism, date rape: are these behaviors of intelligent human beings? Drunkenness may explain behavior but it does not excuse it. Drunks remain responsible for their actions. Trouble can start with the first drink!

Have you wondered why so many high school and college students abuse alcohol so frequently? Research suggests two reasons: one, they see their peers getting drunk, and two, drunkenness is perceived to be OK. In other words, "monkey see, monkey do," and social acceptability. Probably not much will change for the better until more individuals have the courage to stand up for moderation and moral responsibility, no matter how unpopular.

Self-Esteem

I counseled a 19-year-old once.
She was suffering from low self-esteem and was
sinking deeper and deeper. Her parents were
divorced, and she was living with her father.
After our counseling session she would be
returning home to a fast-food meal her father
routinely ordered. She didn't do a thing around
the house; she didn't know how. No wonder
she was in trouble. She spent her time setting
her hair, polishing her nails, and watching TV
soaps, hardly the kind of activities that build
solid self-worth. Before she left that day, I told
her how to cook a simple meal! And I felt sad
for her.

How did we develop self-esteem, that sense
deep within us out of which we believe we are
worthwhile and have value? I think mine

developed because my parents loved me no matter how much I messed up. My teachers convinced me that God loves me, AND parents and teachers together taught me how to do worthwhile things!

Some years ago I read that California and some other states were mandating courses in self-esteem and dropping some math and reading courses. I grew numb! A course or even friendly talk about self-esteem is not the way it develops. Self value grows as a result of three things happening in our lives. 1) We are loved, 2) we have learned to think positively about ourselves, and 3) we have developed some skills. We can do!

I want to emphasize the WE CAN DO! Kids who can solve math problems, write complete sentences, speak English clearly, spell accurately, recite poetry, read intelligently, think logically, debate joyfully, play an instrument, plant and tend a garden, scrub a floor, make their beds, and prepare a simple meal have scores of reasons to feel good about themselves.

It's a serious mistake to substitute a course on self-esteem when that time could be used to develop the artist, poet, scientist, mathematician, musician, friend, storyteller, craftsperson, intellectual, saint in someone.

When we build a home we construct it brick by brick, piece by piece. Something real results. If all we do is talk about building, we end up with nothing but the talk. Self-esteem is built, brick by brick, piece by piece. Don't pass up all the opportunities you have every day to add one of those bricks.

Unexpected Love

I got caught in a lie in my freshman year in high school. What I remember most is that my teacher didn't cast me to the netherworld because I had lied. Nor did he shame me into feeling an inch tall. I knew what I had done was wrong, and I felt bad about it. He could have rejected me, tossed me to the winds, but he didn't. He loved me. He accepted me in spite of my failure, and he apparently cared about me apart from my actions. His love was not conditioned by my behavior. He loved me for me.

I think one reason this incident lingers in my memory is because I didn't expect this kind of caring from a teacher, especially that particular teacher. I am sure I took this kind of love for granted from my parents. After all, they brought me into this world and were stuck with me. They couldn't abandon me, could they? But a teacher, unrelated by blood, part of an institution, an authority figure, one who had every right to discipline me, why should he care that much?

Deep within our Christian belief system is the notion that every person is a precious creation of a loving God, no matter what. We believe that God loves us with unconditional love, God loves us for the WHO, not for the WHAT, we are.

Experiencing the unconditional love of another person is a powerful way in which self-esteem is developed. To actually have someone deeply and genuinely care about you, not for what you do or give or bring, but simply for you, is to have the makings of a deeper self-esteem.

Talking about love is okay, but it will not increase my self-esteem. We have to experience the love of others. Telling ourselves we are okay is not the same as really believing it. Talk is cheap. The payoff is in the doing.

Making A Difference

I couldn't help being inspired.
Wherever on campus I went that December
evening, kids were doing good things. It start-
ed with the prime rib dinner for homeless people. Begun two years earlier by a student, the
event has become a tradition. Assisted by food
service staff, some 30 students organized and
pulled off this year's feast for 150 men, women,
and children who registered through the
Dorothy Day Center and Listening House, two
of our city's shelters.

I sat with two young couples and two
Catholic Charities staffers. The fare was
exquisite, the ambiance celebrative, and the
service most hospitable. A choir comprised of
student volunteers sang Christmas songs till
exhaustion set in (in the singers, that is!). After

downing the richest chocolate cake smothered with raspberry sauce ever concocted, I stole over to the piano and accompanied a motley crew of kids in Rudolph, Silent Night, and other favorites. The party was simple fun!

As I was leaving the building that night, sounds of music from the student lounge drew me in its direction. The floor was full of young people dancing to a D.J.'s best selection. Some appeared to be persons with mental handicaps. Momentarily, Mike, head of "Best Buddies," introduced himself, along with several other student volunteers, and their best buddies. I asked Mike what he got out of his volunteering in this program. His comment pleased my altruistic bones no end. "At first, 18 months ago when I met Jim, my buddy, I felt I was giving a lot. But now that we have become friends, it doesn't feel like I am doing volunteer work anymore. It's great!" And great it is, I thought. This is how it is supposed to work.

When I finally left the student center and headed for home, the sight and sounds of Indians in full costume and bells pulled me toward the field house. In it, more than 2,000 Native Americans were having their annual pow-wow, another way our school serves folks from the community.

I was proud and feeling good when I finally got home that evening. Volunteer activity is inspiring because it changes people's lives so much for the better.

Be A Friend

"To have friends, you have to be a friend." This is advice I was given years ago. It came at a time when I was struggling with the question of friendship, expecting more from friends than I was willing to give myself. It is good advice. On a practical level, it means several things.

First, if you want friends, you have to be friendly. This includes qualities such as hospitality, humor, warmth, courtesy, and genuineness.

Second, if you want to have friends, you have to take some initiative. You cannot be passive and always wait for your friend to call you, invite you, give you a gift. You have to share responsibility for the relationship.

Third, if you want friends, you have to

reveal your inner self. This does not mean everything about yourself! Sharing one's deepest thoughts and feelings and even the secret part of oneself has to be appropriate to the level of the relationship. Nevertheless, sharing one's soul is the basis of friendship.

Fourth, having a friend means mutuality. Mutuality means equality, fairness, justice, a right relationship. One does not use power over another or manipulate or use the friend for personal gain.

Friendship comes in a wide variety of shapes and sizes and depths. It is truly one of God's great and wonderful creations. It is worth working on, and is an accomplishment and gift to cherish. Sometimes it happens naturally, other times it has to be pursued. Either way, it is a treasure.

8

Giving Our Word

Are today's young people afraid of commitment? Do they run from anything that might require permanence, like marriage or priesthood or religious life, for example? Can they be faithful: to spouses, children, nation, neighborhood? How deeply do they value trust, honesty, responsibility, loyalty, fidelity, and promise-keeping?

Good questions, all. Civilizations rise and fall on their outcomes!

In my pastoral ministry, when a marriage has hit hard times and the couple asks for guidance, often I am saddened by the couple's blindness toward each other. He talks about his children as his family, to which he is totally committed. He talks about his wife as though she were "outside" his commitment, the enemy to him and his children, not an equal member of his family. She talks in similar fashion. I stand in amazement. How can it be? Couples who began their marriage committed to each other for life, in sickness and in health, for richer and for poorer, until death, now do not even think of their spouse as part of their FAMILY.

Do we fail to teach, model, preach, and proclaim every wedding as the start of a new family? Surely it is less easy to dissolve a relationship when both parties see themselves as the founders of a new family, with this new family demanding the same loyalty, love, patience, endurance, fidelity, and commitment as the family of origin. Husband and wife are family to each other. Their marriage is founded on mutual promises. They have spoken words of mutual self-giving. This is true even when they bear no children.

The Catholic church is among those religious organizations committed to promoting family values. The commitment to keep one's promise is the "heart" of family. "I give you my word" must remain for every one of us a pact, contract, promise, something that can be trusted and depended upon. If practice makes perfect, maybe this is an area requiring more practice—giving our word and putting our souls and selves behind it.

This is something you might want to think about—beginning now.

God's Law

9

False Gods

"I am the Lord thy God. Thou shalt not have false Gods before me." This is the first of the ten commandments. I haven't seen anyone fall down on their knees to worship a golden calf lately. However, I have on occasion run into people who seem completely immersed in their investments or their possessions. I have met people who are captivated by the pursuit of fame or who are filled with self-indulgence. I suppose it could happen to any of us, human as we are.

These are dramatic examples of "idol" worship, but there is an idolatry of a more subtle type, and possibly more sinister. I'm talking about Christians who know God exists but do not grant God the time of day. Sleep is more important than Sunday Mass. If it isn't sleep, it's jogging, or a paper, or touch football, or whatever.

When I hear folks complain about the increase in crime, the lowering of moral standards in today's world, the upswing in materialism, or how fast the younger or older generation is going to the dogs, I wonder about it all.

Moses had the right idea that long, long time ago. Hey, you want to make the world a better place? Then start with the basics. Polish up the first commandment. PUT GOD FIRST in your life. How can you be sure the rest is in order, if your Creator, Redeemer, and Sanctifier is not the number one priority?

Having no faith is like having a nice looking car, but no fuel. Sunday without worship is like Christmas without Christ. Your life might feel good but something essential is missing. Regular Sunday worship is an effective way to keep your priorities in order.

Believe deeply in the first commandment and watch the values of genuine religion, altruism, moral integrity, and self-esteem grow.

10

First Things First

"Thou shalt not take the name of the Lord, thy God, in vain." This is the second commandment. The philosopher Dietrich von Hildebrand claimed in his book *The Art of Living,* that reverence was the Mother of all virtue. I agree. And the older I get, the more I see his point.

Reverence is the ability to truly know something and to treat it the way it ought to be treated. More simply stated, food is for nourishment, not a food-fight; a chalice is for sacred rituals, not casual meals; the Bible is for uplifting a soul, not a window; friends are for fellowship, not exploitation.

Of all that exists, God is the most profound, most holy reality. God is worthy of our respect. Not to know this is to be ignorant of the most basic truth in life. We were made to know, love, and serve God, and to be happy with our divine creator forever in heaven.

If we want our life to be in proper order, we must put first things first. Treat God as God, not as an easy gimmick to swear by in order to bolster an argument or secure a bet. Don't use God to further falsehood. To trivialize the creator is to do God an irreverence.

Without reverence for God, can one really have reverence for self or others? Can one develop any of the other virtues such as fidelity, justice, honesty, self-respect, or courage?

If we say we want values, and we want to improve the world, there's no better place to start than with a profound reverence for God. It shows up in our language, our priorities, and regular Sunday worship. The spin-offs are obvious. Treat God right and chances are good we will treat ourselves and others right, too.

11

Sunday Priorities

"Remember to keep holy the sabbath day." This third commandment makes me wonder: is one hour a week out of 168 hours too much to give back to God? This question threw me for a loop the first time I heard it. A group of us were arguing about our Catholic obligation to attend Sunday Mass. Obviously, some of us thought it an imposition on our freedom and our life-style.

I admire people who have enough spiritual guts to make Sunday worship a priority. Recently, at a graduation party, I struck up a conversation with a grandma in her 80s. She recalled her father, who, when she was a child, would bundle up the family in their sleigh, and trek seven miles to Mass no matter what the weather was. If it was very bad, he would advise the others to stay at home, and he would walk to Mass, representing them all before God. Hard to believe that today seven blocks is too far for many of us.

The excuses people create to justify ignoring the Source of our life are many. "Too tired." "Got in too late Saturday evening." "Church is too boring." "I'm in my rebellion phase." "God who?" "Religion is for soft-heads." Whatever.

The third commandment is tougher to keep nowadays than when I was young. Sunday has become a major shopping day, but for many it is still a day of rest and relaxation. For Christians it is "The Lord's Day," a celebration of Jesus' resurrection. In our tradition, each Sunday is a "little Easter." Keeping Sundays "holy" is how we "keep the faith."

A strong society is built upon the moral courage and strength of the individuals who make it up. Thank God for people of deep faith. That must be what Jesus meant when he talked about a house built on rock—placing top priority on Sunday worship.

What Is Honor?

"Honor thy father and thy mother." This is the fourth commandment. A teenager's relationship with parents undergoes a gradual but major transformation as he or she merges into adulthood. "Honor" takes on less the meaning of obedience and more the meaning of mutuality, appreciation, and gratitude. Learning to relate to one's parents adult-to-adult becomes a crucial life task.

Parents, for their part, have to let go some, and learn to relate to a young adult who used to be a child and an all-too-independent teenager. For some parents and their young adult offspring, the break is easy and quick. For others, it is difficult and evolves ever so slowly. There is no one right way to work through this process, and no one is exempt from having to do so.

Honor means mutuality. Parents and their young adult sons or daughters must grow in mutual respect, mutual consideration, respect for each other's decisions, and acceptance of differing viewpoints, choices of friends, and life-style decisions. This can require lots of patience and growth in understanding. Honoring also includes forgiving each other for messing up at times.

Honor also means appreciation of what parents have done by way of self-sacrifice, love, and leadership in earlier years. Parenting has never been easy. In the latter part of the 20th century, it has been exceptionally challenging. At any time, nothing delights a parent's heart more than feeling appreciated and being thanked by a son or daughter.

For the young adult, honoring parents also means taking responsibility and caring for them when necessary. No one is perfect and no one is completely self-sufficient, including one's parents. It is a wonderful stage of development toward maturity when the young adult begins to provide adult assistance to his or her parents. The child is no longer a child but an adult, responsive and responsible, exercising care and compassion, and taking the initiative to insure the welfare of his or her elders. We don't have to wait until our parents are eighty to return their love and care!

The fourth commandment means different things at different ages and stages of growth. Over a lifetime, it is a journey from obedience to dependent care. During high school and college years, young adult children learn to relate in exciting and beneficial ways with parents, especially in the ways of friendship.

13

God Is Love

"Thou shalt not kill" is the fifth commandment. In light of this, I have to wonder: is the nation going mad? The daily news is crammed with stories of murder, rape, abusive behavior, war and the planning for it, euthanasia, and other types of violence. We are people at risk of being dulled by the frequency of violence and scarred by its imprint.

When will Christians rise up and say, "No more!"? Our souls have been seared by exploiters, ripped apart by panderers of the public. Video cassettes, movies, and music prey upon our weakness, hoping we won't notice the undertones of violence. It's sick.

Violence is sin, an act against our Creator-God. Murder, rape, and abuse are sins. They violate human dignity. They are shameful before God who is love.

Our society sometimes acts as though there is no God, and therefore, no sin. Police, lawyers, and judges, as well as the perpetrators themselves seem to think violent acts are crimes, not sin. Such deeds are wrong only if the perpetrator gets caught, is convicted and punished. Not so. Sin is sin whether or not the sinner gets caught. Wrong is wrong, ever and always. God knows what is in someone's heart, no matter what a jury might decide. The moral order is above the legal order. Ultimately, each person must answer to God.

A sense of sin and faith in God are the best ways to build a world where peace and justice reign. What is missing today is belief in a God who knows us intimately and a sense of personal responsibility for one's sinful behavior.

Crime rates will not diminish until more and more people return to God and believe again in the Ten Commandments. The real answer is not more prisons, more sophisticated home security systems, more police. The real answer is in what people believe. If everyone believed deeply in the fifth commandment, violence would decline and the values of human life, personal dignity, and heartfelt repentance would increase.

Belief in a loving God is the beginning of Wisdom! It is also the foundation for a sound social order.

14

Nothing Hurts as Much

The sixth commandment is "Thou shalt not commit adultery." Nothing hurts quite as badly as infidelity. It violates trust, disrupts the marriage bond, and can leave a family in ruins. Marriage and family are two of God's most precious gifts. No wonder God protects family with all Ten Commandments, and marriage specifically with two of them (the sixth and the ninth).

The sexual appetite is strong and for that reason demands self-control. And self-control doesn't happen without a lot of practice. That is why Christianity has for centuries required abstinence outside of marriage. The New Testament is clear: adultery is sinful. So is fornication. Why? Because they violate marriage and family, and they put pleasure and self-indulgence before fidelity and chastity.

Since the sexual revolution of the 1960s, some things have improved. Sexual information is more accurate and available. Generally people are less uptight, less traumatized by the topic. But some things have deteriorated. Sex has become, for many, an end in itself, divorced from meaningful love. And grown adults, sometimes caught up in their own confusion about sex, cannot summon the courage to require abstinence from the young.

Christians are called to love maturely. The moral context for sex requires honesty, mutual respect, and the commitment of marriage. It also must follow the norm of right relationship to avoid exploitation and abuse by one in a power relationship over another (parent-child, for example, or doctor-patient).

This is no easy task in our sex-saturated, sexually exploitive society. But it is all the more compelling. Believe deeply in the sixth commandment and reap the benefits of chaste love, a faithful marriage, and fulfilling and mutually beneficial friendships. Self-sacrificing love, self-control, and a capacity for genuine intimacy are values that this commandment promotes—countercultural to be sure, but so what? All the more reason to believe in Christian values.

15

Give It Back

"Thou shalt not steal" is the seventh commandment. My father told me to give the nickel back. "It's not yours," he repeated, "you give it back right now!" I rushed over to the corner grocery store to level the scales of justice. You see, the cashier had mistakenly given me an extra nickel.

A nickel, five cents, what's the big deal? The big deal is that little things lead to bigger things. Dishonesty in whatever quantity is still dishonest. Remember the story about the Dutch boy who prevented a dike from collapsing by stopping the trickle with his finger? An ounce of prevention equals a pound of cure. Why the crying need these days for seminars, courses, books, and lectures on ethics?

Consider how many customers and even

employees steal stores blind. Owners must add to the price of goods either to cover their losses on stolen merchandise, or to pay for extra security devices and personnel. Nuts, I say. I would rather live in a world where people can trust each other. But how do we get back to that?

I believe that it starts at home, is continued in school, and moves out into the community. Let's hear it for Dad. That nickel was a big deal!

And let's hear it for the seventh commandment. Hey, you steal something, the sin isn't forgiven until you make restitution. That's what our faith teaches: RESTI-TUTION. Pay it back, level the scales, if it isn't yours you have no right to it. Pretty simple!

Believe in the Seventh Commandment and watch the values of trust, peace of soul, and justice abound.

16

Tell the Truth

Here is the eighth commandment. "Thou shalt not bear false witness against thy neighbor." It is a sin to lie, to "bear false witness." We bear false witness when we falsify documents, tell an untruth, deny responsibility for our actions, willfully mislead another, or distort facts for our own gain.

To the young, truth is not always a major priority. Other things appear more important, such as avoiding punishment, fooling someone else, getting the reward, or saving face. Developing the virtue of honesty can be a tough task for adolescents and young adults. Lying is the easy way out, the most attractive option.

As we grow older, we realize the value of telling the truth. "Honesty is the best policy," my father used to say. One benefit is that truth-tellers do not need to cover up after themselves. Often one lie leads to another. Another benefit is that it is easier to recall the truth, since it really happened. Also, too, being honest is a great way to respect other people.

But honesty requires courage, and courage is hard. It takes courage to face the truth, to look in the mirror at the reflection of our not-so-pretty selves. Yes, it takes courage.

The eighth commandment protects some precious values: trust and truth, mutual respect, and the bonds that bring a community together. We all need to recommit ourselves to telling the truth. It's the only way to go.

17

Wrong Desires

Have you ever "coveted" anything? "Thou shalt not covet thy neighbor's wife" is the ninth commandment. Did you ever want your favorite food so badly, you could taste it? If the thing was not a "thing" at all, but another's girlfriend/boyfriend, and if the desire was so strong it was wrong, you possibly were guilty of "coveting."

Covet is not a word we use everyday, but it is a daily kind of experience. When Jimmy Carter was President, he got himself into a public relations mess by his utterly honest admission that, sure, he was human, he had lusted after a woman other than his wife. He was admitting to having had "covetous" thoughts. Frankly and personally, I was impressed by his honesty. And his courage.

Along with the sixth commandment, the ninth protects marriage and family. It acknowledges that the most powerful sex organ in the human body is the mind. That is where it starts, that is where nature has deposited the chemical sparkplug. And that is also the locus of control.

Think wholesome thoughts and you will do wholesome things. "An idle mind is the devil's workshop," is an old saying that expresses the same idea. Put this in the context of the shows you watch on TV, the soaps, movies, sitcoms. They endorse immoral behaviors, which once rehearsed in our imaginations, no longer seem far-fetched or repugnant. Extramarital affairs can seem so right on the tube! Beware the mental dress rehearsal!

The ninth commandment invites us to cherish the values of marriage and family, responsible sexuality, fidelity, and chastity. Let's recommit ourselves to deeply believing in these values and the commandment which protects them.

18

Greedy Hearts

And finally we come to the tenth commandment. "Thou shalt not covet thy neighbor's goods." How strong must your desire be for someone else's stuff before it is sinful? You mean a person can sin just by thinking, merely by desiring or wanting something?

The tenth commandment goes after that kind of "wrongful thinking and desiring," which is like stockpiling dynamite. True, it may never go off, but adding explosives to the pile makes the neighborhood more dangerous!

For example, let's say I want something so strongly I would cheat, steal, lie, even harm another to get it. I have no right to it in the first place. Yet my desire for this something is so intense my moral balance is off-kilter, my conscience is in a tailspin, and I desire what I know to be wrong.

Greed, envy, jealousy, hate, and lust are all cousins to covetousness. They travel together. They like each other's company. Borrowing a phrase from AA, coveting is "stinking thinking." It is a crime waiting to happen, a mind corrupted by desire to which it has no right— no right, perhaps, but plenty of might. A coveting mind can have a powerful impact on one's behavior.

Believing in the tenth commandment and abiding by it is a way to maintain respect for other people's property. It also helps us avoid the self-destructiveness a greedy heart assuredly causes, and it prevents us from going off the deep end because of envy or jealousy. Follow this commandment and watch the values of trust, mutual respect, humility, and honesty grow.

Postscript to the Commandments

Jesus was asked one day which of the commandments was the greatest. His response was instructional. "Love God with all your heart, all your mind, and all your soul. That is the first. The second is like it: Love your neighbor as yourself!" Jesus boiled down the ten to two, and they, in turn, boil down to one word, love. Love is the great commandment.

Love means reverence for God, self, and others. Love is at the heart of every commandment. Whether we follow the ten from Moses, or the Great ONE from Jesus, it is the same. It is the call from God to learn how to truly love.

Love is, indeed, as the old song says, what makes the world go 'round.

STRAIGHT TALK ABOUT
Faith

19

Close the Gap

How well do you know Jesus? If not well, it's time to remedy that deficiency in your spiritual life. It's time to fill the hole, close the gap. Decide now to develop what should be the most significant relationship in your life.

To discover the person of Jesus, look for him in your Bible. With a note pad and pencil at your fingertips, slowly "walk through" one of the four gospels. As you read, jot down words that describe Jesus, his personality, priorities, likes and dislikes, moods, actions, and desires. Make a summary list of his most important teachings.

Achieving this much will take several hours, but it will be time well spent. Each time you do this conclude with a prayer. Close your eyes, be silent, imagine that you are speaking with

Jesus. Talk with him about what you read. Express your feelings, ask your questions, state your ideas.

Developing a personal relationship with Jesus, as with any relationship, takes time. To have Jesus as a friend, you have to be a friend with him. This simply means spending time, taking an interest in, caring about, sharing honestly and deeply, trusting, giving and receiving.

Friendship with Jesus is a real possibility because God has given us the gift of the Holy Spirit. The Spirit of Jesus lives in the hearts of believers and is not limited by time or space or physical form. Many Christians know Jesus as a personal friend, and they experience their relationship as both supportive and rewarding. To know Jesus is to know God.

My prayer for you is that you will take the time to form just such a relationship—and that you will come to know God very well indeed.

20

Times Have Changed

When I was a kid, Sunday was big. We got strong values on Sundays. In church, fidelity, love, and honesty were drilled into us. So was respect: for self, for other people, and for other people's property. We learned the value of sacrifice for others. It's better to give than receive, better to die a hero than to live a coward. Don't ask what your church can do for you—ask what you can do for your church!

In my home, Sunday Mass was a top priority, followed by the family. Relatives didn't have to telephone before dropping in to visit because they knew they were welcome anytime. Not only was everyone usually home for family dinner, the kids hung around afterwards and actually enjoyed their parents' company. Later we visited our grandparents—all of us!

And we did no "servile" work. Sunday was a day of rest. Except for emergencies, it was wrong to cut lawns, paint the house, clean closets, go to the office, hire out to the neighbors. The stores were all closed, so shopping was an impossibility. Like I said, Sunday was for God and family.

Today, we are bombarded by a whole different set of values. Sundays are now "valued" for sales and discounts. The masses are at the malls more than in the churches. Family dinner? What's that? Visit relatives? You gotta be kidding; they're out shopping, too. No work on Sunday? Crazy, man, half the teenagers in town work on Sundays. It's important to the economy! They are big spenders.

So this is what a materialistic, secular society is like. For my money, the old days seemed a lot better. Faith had a chance then because worship was given top priority. And family had a chance because it came in a very close second.

What ever happened to the third commandment? Yes, times have changed. But as difficult as it might be, it is still important to find ways to promote worship of God and to experience family life. Struggle as we must, it is critical to put religion in first place with family close behind.

21

God Deserves the Best!

"It makes me proud to be a Catholic." A man in mid-life said this to me recently. He was grateful for the strong, forthright leadership taken by the American Catholic bishops on the controversial and complicated issues of abortion, war and peace, and the economy. Our conversation quickly jumped to Pope John Paul and his influence on the crumbling of the Berlin Wall and thawing of the cold war.

More recently, Christian leaders have been in the news negotiating for peace in Peru, sheltering the homeless in cities across America, comforting people in prayer at times of tragedy, providing hope in peaceful resolution of conflict throughout Eastern Europe and elsewhere. The list is long. Christian leaders, Protestant and Catholic, on the side of justice, compassion, truth, freedom, and human dignity.

When I was in high school, the brightest and the best students with the most potential were encouraged to become leaders within the church. Some of the brightest and best did pursue ecclesial careers. Most of us seemed pretty average. All of us, I think, believed the church deserved our best.

God deserved the best then, God deserves the best now. The best of us and the best the "average" person can offer. Our world needs strong leadership from the church. To provide it, the church needs strong leaders from among its members.

It's not easy being a leader. It never was, never will be. Expectations often are unreasonable, human weaknesses all too obvious. Yet, the need is urgent for leaders with moral courage, wisdom, a willingness to sacrifice self, and a deep commitment to build a better world.

Our parishes and institutions are loaded with Christian leaders, actual and potential. Faith-filled leaders make an exceptional impact upon the course of human history. Our world awaits your YES!

22

Christ and Christmas

The struggle is ongoing. How to keep Christ in the celebration of Christmas? The answer is faith and perseverance. For Christians, this holiday season is first and foremost a holy season. It's a celebration of the divine-human wedding of the transcendent Omnipotence becoming a humble Immanence. Translated this means that God dwells with us and within us.

Christmas is pregnant with meaning. Humans hunger for union with God, for peace, and for wholeness, and Christmas reminds us that these hungers can be satisfied. The four weeks preceding December 25th have traditionally been a time for personal prayer and reflection. The Old Testament readings from Isaiah are exquisite meditations for our spiritual growth. They feed the imagination, stretching the heart to yearn ever more deeply for the God who is the Source of life and love, the God who is our Emmanuel, that is, "God-with-us."

Christmas is a powerful feast because it's a love feast. God is Love, and perhaps there is no more powerful realization than that God indeed loves "me," loves "you," loves all of us personally.

The tragedy in the way our culture insists on celebrating Christmas is that so many of us get caught up, much too soon, in the shopping and decorating and partying. Before the merchandise tycoons took over the season, Christians had a simpler time of it. They used the season of Advent to pray and wait and long for God. The celebration did not begin until Christmas Eve and then it continued for the twelve days after Christmas.

The key in our culture, I propose, is for Christians to persevere in the heroic effort to keep the holy in the holiday, to keep Christ in Christmas, to make sure the spiritual dimension is realized before accommodating oneself to the preferences of a secular culture. The secular is not all bad. There is a celebrative tone to it all. Keeping one's balance in the rushing commercial river is the challenge. Faith and perseverance definitely help.

May God bless us all as we strive to touch and be touched by our God, not just at Christmas, but every day of our lives.

23

Plans for Lent

Lent is a God-given time. It helps us keep our priorities straight. It is a time to reflect about who we are in relation to God and others. It's a time to focus on a right relationship with God. For centuries, Christians have viewed Lent as a time to strengthen that relationship. It is also a time to give something special to an uncertain world, and to deepen our prayer life.

If you haven't yet decided what you are going to do this Lent, might I recommend Plan A (10 minutes a day) or Plan B (an hour a week).

Plan A (One of the following daily):
•Find a Bible passage over which to ponder and pray

•Use a prayer book daily
•Meditate about how to be more positive to some-
one who irritates you
•Contemplate God's Presence in your favorite
prayer setting
•Pray with a friend
•Talk with God in regular morning or evening
prayer

Plan B (One of the following at least once a week):
•Attend Mass
•Pray the Stations of the Cross
•Volunteer with an agency that helps the needy
•Spend an extra hour with someone who is sad,
lonely, or afraid
•Study one hour longer in an effort to do your
best at your studies

24

About Marriage

This one particular couple stands out in my mind. They expressed such a strong belief in marriage as a sacrament. The groom-to-be was explicit. "We know that marriage is a sacrament and we are entering it with that in mind." It was obvious that he and his bride-to-be were preparing themselves for a grace-filled encounter with Christ. It was refreshing to witness such faith.

Later, at the reception, I talked to the bride's mother. "When my husband and I got married we believed that marriage was a sacrament. I think these kids (the bride and groom) believe that marriage is something special because it's a sacrament." Aha, I thought. The acorn doesn't fall far from the tree. These kids were blessed by the strong Catholic faith of their parents.

Not a bad way to begin a marriage.

Marriage is a sacrament, a visible sign of Christ's love and presence. Husband and wife believe they are sacrament, instruments of faith through which God blesses them and all who are touched by their positive example. A sacrament is something special in our Catholic faith.

Marriage is an expression of the covenant relationship between God and the couple. It's something the couple is, it's something they continue to become, a visible sign of God's love and presence for all the rest of us.

When a couple believes they make their vows in God's presence, that God will be with them in their life journey together, and that they are called to be a "little church," a "home church," a dwelling-place for God's Spirit, they are being sacrament to each other and to the world about them. This kind of thinking and believing takes time—just as a solid relationship does. Marriage is not a spur of the moment act. It is a lifetime commitment.

25

The Call to Priesthood

There we were, forty of us. We were on retreat, and the youngest was ordained only three years, the oldest ordained fifty-two. Together the forty of us have logged 1,412 years of loving service to the Catholic church! That translates into better than a half-million days of ministry.

My mind wandered in wonder at the realization of this. Ordained to be "other Christs," this quiet bunch of guys has done its best to prepare themselves and others for the church of the next millennium. I am proud to be in their number.

The priesthood is a call to commitment, compassion, and courage. It is a call to commitment in a time when many others are avoiding it; a call to compassion in a culture that glorifies self-indulgence; a call to courage in a time when it is not easy to be a religious leader who preaches a gospel way of life.

Priesthood is as noble, as good, as special as any career or calling. Try as this world does to discredit and deny religion's role, the fact remains: Jesus called apostles to total service, and he asks no less of today's priests. For Catholics, bishops and priests have truly significant responsibility for leadership. The church has a right to the best we can give.

I know there are vocations out there. There are people who are capable of commitment, compassion, and courage. And capable of something more—sacrifice. In an era where pleasure is highlighted, celibacy seems too much to be asked. In a time of attractive materialism, gospel simplicity appears old-fashioned and irrational.

No question about it. Celibacy and simplicity are countercultural. They require a willingness to forgo one thing for the sake of something else. Not an easy choice to make, but one that blesses us all.

26

What about Sin?

Confession? Who goes anymore?
Who needs it? Who sins anymore? When he was 80, psychiatrist Karl Menninger wrote the book *Whatever Became of Sin?* This internationally famous doctor saw a shift taking place in American culture which he seriously questioned. It was the movement away from calling what is wrong "wrong," and sin "sin." The fashion was (and still is) to call moral wrong and sin "inappropriate behavior!" Menninger, a faithful Christian, deplored this shift and called for a return to the basic Christian understanding of good and evil.

Calling moral wrong "sin" puts us before our Maker and acknowledges our actual responsibility before God for our actions. Trying to soften reality eventually backfires.

Adultery is more than an "indiscretion." Abusive treatment is more than "inappropriate behavior." Fraud, embezzlement, and theft are not merely "crimes." They are moral wrongs. In plain old-fashioned but accurate words they are sin. And to be healed, we have to ask for and receive God's forgiveness.

Think about it. If we call theft a crime only, and not a sin as well, it puts the burden on the police, not on us. In other words, "I'm home free as long as I don't get caught!" If I act with this attitude, the responsibility is subtly but falsely lifted from my shoulders—where it belongs—to someone else's. If we call sin an indiscretion or an inappropriate behavior, we acknowledge only part of reality. We deny God's rightful role in our lives. We pretend God has no place in our daily existence.

So what does confession (also known as the sacrament of reconciliation) do for us? It helps us deal with the total reality, name the sin, avoid the evasions, accept responsibility for our lives, acknowledge our weakness before an understanding Creator, and receive God's powerful gift of mercy. Confession is healthy for the soul. It helps us deal with the full reality of our lives, of which sin is a part.

Love and Sexuality

27

Intimacy

I have lived a celibate existence all my life. I was asked recently by a young 24-year-old husband and father of three, how I do it. I replied that since it's intimacy, not sex, that is the essential human need, I was satisfied and did not feel humanly deprived. Besides, my friends and my prayer life provide an intimacy with other people and with God.

Intimacy is the feeling of closeness, the sense of being one with another person in mind and heart. Humans can scarcely survive without intimacy. And intimacy is the result of people sharing their stories, discussing their values, caring for one another, opening their vulnerable side to the other, sharing their lives, their joy, their pain. Intimacy is never accomplished in a one-night stand. It is won gradually, evolving over time as shared experiences weave tighter bonds and develop closer ties.

Intimacy is the experience of "oneness of soul." It happens in a variety of dimensions. Intimacy can be:

Intellectual: when two people think alike, or feel bonded because of sharing poetry, ideas, thoughts, even enjoying lively debate!

Emotional: when people sense a closeness because they share affection and common feelings (hopes, fears, joys, pain, excitement, etc.)

Social: when people feel a oneness as a group, or team, club, or organization. Close friends who like to socialize together.

Moral: when people feel deeply united because of shared principles and moral values and work together for a cause.

Spiritual: when people feel at one in prayer, sharing common beliefs, customs, rituals, and traditions.

Physical: when people are united physically by holding hands, giving affectionate hugs, or as sexual partners.

No question about sex being one of God's gifts, and a wonderful one at that. But having sex is no guarantee that the human need for intimacy will be fulfilled. Humans fulfill their intimacy needs in a variety of ways, only one of which is physical.

28

Adolescent Sex

"Wait until marriage." This is not a popular message these days, but nevertheless it's a very wise choice. Sexual activity requires the maturity of an adult and can be fraught with danger when engaged in prematurely. What follows is a list of six reasons for abstinence (not to mention the Christian moral standard for the unmarried):

•Adolescents are not ready to be parents, and the only one hundred percent effective method for preventing pregnancy is abstinence.

•Genital sexual intimacy has emotional and psychological consequences far beyond what youth are capable of handling. Sex requires a maturity level that they don't yet have. (This fact is not a "put-down" of young people, it's the way God created human nature.)

•Non-exploitive sex can only be assured between two adults who have a mature sense of self and well-developed moral values. Adolescents are especially vulnerable to sexual exploitation because their identities and moral values are still very much in the formative stage. Physical readiness precedes emotional and moral readiness by several years!

•AIDS and sexually transmitted diseases are prevented most certainly by reserving genital sex for your marriage partner who has also waited for you. The 100% effective method of preventing these calamities is for two people to abstain from sex until they are in a committed, monogamous, and faithful relationship with a disease-free partner.

•The best way to avoid feeling pressured to have an abortion, or "having to get married," or having to get tested for AIDS and STDs, is to choose abstinence.

•We have to learn to crawl before we can walk, and learn to walk before we can run. Genital sex is like the running stage. Before two persons are ready for sex, they must learn well the lessons of friendship, responsibility, mature communication, and self-discipline. Waiting until marriage forces a couple to work on the relationship.

Christian moral standards for genital sexual activity call for maturity, trust, responsibility, fidelity, and love. This is a wise moral teaching gained from centuries of experience, one young adults have a right not only to hear, but to practice.

29

Living Together

Virginity before marriage? Yes, there is no better way. This "old fashioned" practice is slowly gaining popularity once again.

Though many continue to believe that cohabitation is a good way to prepare for marriage, statistics don't bear that out. Recent studies show that divorce is more likely for couples who lived together before marriage than those who didn't. Living together without the benefit of legal and religious bonds puts the couple in a fragile and false relationship. Expecting to be able to really get to know one another ("so we can find out whether we should get married," they say), their "pretend" marriage forces them to hold back something of their real selves.

One of the advantages marriage has over

cohabitation is that it provides husband and wife a solid foundation and the freedom for both to be their true selves, trusting in the bond that can "never be broken." Marriage provides the setting, the opportunity, and the encouragement to live in truth rather than in "pretend." Love can only grow if it is based on truth. What wisdom in the Christian moral tradition! Sex is too good and too emotionally charged a gift from a caring God to be taken lightly.

More and more, those who are trying to reverse the destructive trends of our times—pregnancies out of wedlock, abortion, AIDS and other sexually transmitted diseases—realize that the "old morality" which maintains that sex belongs only in marriage is the best way to live.

There is a popular story about a grandpa who was talking with his adolescent grandson and they got onto the topic of sexuality education. The grandson asked his grandpa how they dealt with "STDs" back when he was a kid. Grandpa recalled the answer was simple—a wedding ring! No sex outside of marriage.

The only 100 percent sure-proof method of staying free from the pain and struggles of pregnancies out of wedlock, sexually transmitted diseases, the temptation to have an abortion, and the trauma of AIDS is to save genital sex for marriage.

30

Peer Pressure

What is it that really changes behavior? For years I labored in the field of sexuality education, attempting among other things to prevent teen pregnancies. I believed the experts who said, "Education was the answer," not only to this social dilemma, but to abusive drinking, smoking, sexual abuse, and drunk driving. "If it's a problem," they said, "it can be solved by someone developing a learning module and mandating it."

No question about it, education does do some good. But knowledge and virtue are not the same. Because we know something to be wrong doesn't mean we will not do it.

So, in addition to education, is the answer more laws? They help, but only if they are enforced and their sanctions catch people's attention!

Add to education and laws some effective formation in positive values, and the formula for success improves. Values are not taught so much as formed, therefore, they must be required by someone (usually a parent or other authority) until they have become internalized. Since this process is rarely accomplished before age thirty, teens and "twentysomethings" still need some "requiring" if formation is to be effective.

Then there's the reality of social pressure. Who would have thought a few years ago, for example, that such extensive behavioral changes were possible as have occurred with smoking? A behavior which formerly was "cool," but now ostracizes, stigmatizes, and shuns one into shame becomes much easier to give up or avoid!

Many educational institutions are doing an adequate job with sexuality education. But formation is another matter. Until families, churches, schools, youth organizations of all types, and society in general say NO, and back it up with values formation (which is far more than either values clarification or even education about values) and some laws holding parents and teens more accountable, we will not see adolescent sexual activity rates decline.

The final factor that must be in place is the social pressure factor. Adolescent sex must become, once again, a behavior that is not acceptable by society, by parents and other adults, or by youth themselves. This is the next sexual revolution that must happen if our society is to survive the threat of adolescent premature sex.

31

Men Who Rape

What is your image of a rapist?

Did you know that most rapes are committed by "normal guys" with women they know? The stereotype that rapists are usually strangers, masked villains who jump out of bushes and attack, is false. Surveys of college campuses reveal startling statistics: one in four women surveyed were victims of rape or attempted rape. Eighty-four percent of those raped knew their attacker. Fifty-seven percent of the rapes happened on dates.

Nine out of ten victims never report the rape. Very few decide to prosecute. And the male's problem escalates. Yes, the male's problem. Rape is a serious problem behavior, and it won't be solved or improved until men get off the dime and do something about their attitudes and behaviors.

MS Magazine recently studied 32 college campuses. Of the students surveyed, eight percent admitted having raped or attempted to rape a woman. These young men differed from non-assaultive males in several ways: they drank and got drunk more often, reported more family violence at home, talked daily with their friends about how pleasurable particular women "would be in bed," and were frequent readers of *Playboy*-type magazines.

They also believed that prevention of rape was the woman's responsibility, and they considered aggression a normal part of sex.

Thank God most men are not rapists. The vast majority of males are decent human beings and respect women. Even so, men need to learn more about rape, especially acquaintance rape, and take more initiative to make the world a safer place.

You can change the world you live in! Don't tolerate attitudes, speech, or behavior from friends or acquaintances who show disrespect for women. Have the courage to speak out against "locker-room" talk! If something sounds exploitive or looks exploitive, it probably is. "Macho" is out! Respect is in. Review again the characteristics of assault-prone males. If the description fits you, you could be dangerous!

32

Acquaintance Rape

Acquaintance rape is preventable.
Well, maybe not always, but some of the time.
Rape is never the victim's fault. Still, some
things can be done to increase the likelihood of
prevention. One thing that helps is for women
to be cautious about men who exhibit certain
behaviors. Robin Warshaw, in *I Never Called It
Rape* lists several characteristics of acquaintance rapists:

- He insults, belittles, ignores your opinion
  (emotional abuse)
- Likes to control you (needs to approve
  your friends, your dress, and other ele-
  ments of your life and relationships)
- Talks negatively about women
- Gets jealous when there is no reason
- Uses drugs or gets drunk or tries to get you
  intoxicated

- •Berates you for not wanting to get high, have sex, or accompany him to an isolated spot
- • Refuses to let you share any expenses on a date (buys you)
- • Is physically violent or pushy
- • Acts in an intimidating way toward you
- • Gets angry when sexually or emotionally frustrated
- • Doesn't view you as an equal; has a fascination with weapons
- • Enjoys being cruel to animals, children, or people he can bully.

In addition to avoiding the men with these characteristics, the author also recommends that women do the following:

- •Set sexual limits and communicate those limits
- •Be assertive
- •Stay sober
- •Remain in control
- •Find out beforehand about a person before going on a date
- •Don't assume others will take care of you
- •Trust your feelings.

Students, especially freshmen, should take special precaution. The most dangerous time is between move-in day and the first holiday break, a period when freshman women are most vulnerable. Become informed, discuss this issue with friends, and be intentional about avoiding risky situations.

STRAIGHT TALK ABOUT
Virtues

33

Let Goodness Guide You

Will Steger is a renowned polar explorer. He has traversed by dogsled both the Arctic and Antarctic regions. I recently heard Will describe his adventures. I listened with amazement, awestruck at the challenges nature hurled at him, his teammates, and their dogs.

What is it that drives explorers like Will to push on, withstanding months of frigid air, blinding snowstorms, and danger lurking at every footstep? Every day was a series of brushes with death, and there was nowhere to turn but to the resources on hand and the courage within.

When someone in the audience asked him what made him tick, Will Steger told in simple terms of a childhood driven by a desire to explore and of parents who tolerated, if not encouraged, his adventurous spirit. He described, too, his love of the environment, God's creation, the Earth. In chilling terms he warned of the ozone's depletion, in words all too much like doomsday talk. "Your generation," he told the young folks, "will be forced to make the tough decisions needed to save this planet." The time is short.

"What can we do?" someone else asked. "Start in simple ways," Will said, "by conserving and recycling, by pushing for protection of the environment, however you can."

"What principles guide your life?" another inquired. "Goodness," he said. "Always seek goodness as the first rule. Second, surround yourself with positive people. You can survive negative people only for a while—eventually they influence you! Third, the answers are within. Look deep inside yourself when you face difficult challenges. God is there." These are wise words from one who has lived on the edge of danger, who has been forced, again and again, to find answers within himself in the midst of crises! They are words that fit us, too. Let's take them to heart.

34

Be Courageous

"Not acting" can be very cowardly. If you have information about another person who is stealing, cheating, vandalizing, or doing other seriously destructive actions and you fail to notify the proper authorities, you share in that person's wrongdoing. In following the "code of silence," you contribute to the destruction of trust in the community; you shatter the morale of others. Your refusal to right a wrong may be an irresponsible "caving in" to peer pressure. It takes courage to rise above the harmful code of silence. If you think you have a moral obligation to speak up, but aren't sure, seek the advice of a wise counselor. Weakness rules when courage is lacking. Be a contributor. Add to the community's morale by not allowing negative people to exercise negative control. Have courage!

35

Practice Tolerance

Occasionally it happens. An African, Asian, or Hispanic American, or other person of color, receives an ugly phone call or a hate letter or a violent threat of some kind. Nothing saddens me more. In our society there can be no room for hatred, for racial prejudice, for violence to the dignity of each person. Every human person is a creation of God and possesses a dignity that no one has a right to deny. Prejudice is small-minded and mean. Whenever we are confronted by it, we have no choice but to challenge it and set it right. Never be tolerant of prejudice. It acts as a poison threatening everything healthy and whole. Be a contributor. Christian love must prevail. Love's victory is in your hands.

36

Show Integrity

"You are what you eat." This is a common slogan. Eat junk food and your body will show it. The same is true of your mind. Feed it trashy books, lots of violence, exploitive fantasies, lusty thoughts, and your mind will show it. We were made for purposes more noble than the lowest common denominators in life. Porn is not okay even though it sells and enough people want it. Promiscuous sex is not okay even though movie and sports stars brag about it. Porn, violence, greed, and lust are destroyers. God didn't make junk when we were created. And God didn't make us to become junk through choices of our own. The choice is ours! To be or not to be...a person of integrity! Be a contributor. Add to the community's morale by keeping healthy physically and spiritually.

37

Keep Commitments

Some people like to leave their options open. You ask for a date, she always hems and haws wondering whether a better offer is pending. You need a volunteer, he's always booked. You expect marriage vows to be forever, he or she has an unspoken list of "causes for divorce." It takes guts, courage, and perseverance to make a commitment, especially a lifelong one. Marriage is tough enough when both spouses have made a lifelong commitment. How much tougher when one or other holds back on the commitment. Lifelong commitment is essential for marriage and family to survive. It's the commitment that makes true love possible; it's the commitment that keeps a family whole. If you are looking for a successful marriage and family, find a partner who is able and willing to make a real commitment.

38

Be Good Stewards

Stewardship is another odd word. And yet we are all stewards in many ways, particularly over our own lives. A young man, considering suicide, told me once: "It's my life, I can do anything with it I want!" Wrong! Your life is not your own, it is God's gift to you. You do not have the right to do just anything you want with a gift. You must respect the intention of the giver. We are obligated to respect life and treat it with profound reverence. It's the same with everything else— as Christians we are stewards of all God's gifts. Everything we own, possess, use, or have is really God's and we are privileged for a time to care for it. Get with the program; each one of us is accountable to God for how we use or abuse the people and the things in our lives. Be a contributor. Add to the community's moral tone by being a good steward, by respecting life and its opportunities.

39

Show Reverence

Reverence is an odd word today. Yet reverence is the foundation of moral character. If you lack respect for God, yourself, or others, you have a serious problem. Get help! Lack of respect shows up in abusive alcohol or drug use, destruction of property, risky behavior, and rough treatment of yourself or other people. In a Christian community, members strive to develop a reverent attitude toward God and all created things, especially persons. A lack of respect has a devastating impact on morale and the common good. Be a contributor. Add to the community's strength by having genuine reverence for everyone and everything, beginning with yourself.

40

Respect Yourself

You are made in God's image. So am I. So are we all. Somehow, for some reason, couched in the infinite mystery of the creator's purpose, human beings reflect their maker. Jesus taught that every person has incredible dignity, and deserves to be respected, even reverenced. His Golden Rule was: treat others as you would want to be treated—with respect. Respect begins with oneself. St. Paul taught that we are temples of God, God lives within the human heart. What greater motivation for reverence for self and others could we have than that? As a popular poster in the 1960s put it: God made me and God doesn't make junk!

Of Related Interest...

Making Moral Choices
An Introduction
Mark Miller, C.Ss.R.
Based in ethical theory, this book summarizes how and why people make moral choices and guides readers toward making good choices. Discussion questions help readers apply the material to their own experiences.   ISBN: 0-89622-666-2, 96 pages, $9.95 (order M-50)

Becoming a Man
Basic Information, Guidance, and Attitudes on Sex for Boys
William J. Bausch
Father Bausch successfully bridges the challenging chasm between gospel values and media models, church teachings and peer pressure. This book is the answer to the prayers of parents, teachers, and guidance counselors for a balanced, comprehensive, and clear approach to sex education and information for young men.
ISBN: 0-89622-357-4, 324 pp, $9.95 (order W-19)

Becoming a Woman
Valerie Dillon
Sensitively written with her own daughter in mind, Dillon uses stories and real life situations to give facts, information, and practical suggestions for dealing with the problems and joys of growing up female. A very helpful guide for teachers and parents
ISBN: 0-89622-433-3, 168 pp, $9.95 (order C-29)

Weekly Prayer Services for Teenagers
Lectionary-Based for the School Year (Years A and B)
M. Valerie Schneider, SND
These 37 prayer services involve teenagers in a dramatic reading of Scripture and include questions for reflection and discussion, a time for communal prayer, and an activity. All are related to a theme associated with the lectionary reading for the week. Themes cover generosity, forgiveness, sacrifice, discipleship, holiness, academics, baptismal commitment, liturgical seasons, and more.
ISBN: 0-89622-692-1, 104 pp, $12.95 (order M-72)
also available in Years B & C
ISBN: 0-89622-732-4, 112 pp, $12.95 (order B-34)

Available at religious bookstores or from:

TWENTY-THIRD PUBLICATIONS
P.O. Box 180 • Mystic, CT 06355

For a complete list of quality books and videos call:
1 - 8 0 0 - 3 2 1 - 0 4 1 1